50 FRENCH PHRASES

Catherine Bruzzone and Susan Martineau

Illustrations by Leighton Noyes
French adviser: Marie-Thérèse Bougard

Contents

Special note for learners!

The key French phrases you will learn are numbered on each spread. There are also extra words you will need for the activities. By the end of the book you will know 50 FRENCH PHRASES and many useful French words. There is a summary of all these at the back of the book.

Pronouncing French

The simple pronunciation guide will help, but it cannot be completely accurate. Read the words as if they were English. Put the stress on the letters in *italics*, for example, boh-*shjoor*. Don't pronounce the "h" at the end of a word, for example, "leh," which is French for "the." If possible, ask for help from a French-speaking person and try to speak on your own as soon as you can.

Bonjour!

Have fun saying hello and good-bye in French. You need to match the right greeting to the pictures, according to the time of day illustrated. Say the correct phrase out loud. You can check your answers on page 32.

1

Bonjour
boh-*shjoor*
Hello,
good morning

2

Au revoir
oh r'*vwahr*
Good-bye

3

Bonsoir
boh-*swahr*
Good evening

4

Bonne nuit
bon nwee
Goodnight

Words to Know

Salut!
sal*oo*
Hi!

À bientôt
ah bee-an-*toh*
See you soon

le jour
leh shjoor
day

le soir
leh swahr
evening

la nuit
lah nwee
night

Je m'appelle...

Ask your friends or family to play this naming game with you.
One person needs to be blindfolded and spun around. Then he
or she has to "find" someone and ask **Comment tu t'appelles?**
The person answers **Je m'appelle...** and says **Et toi?** Take
turns being the "finder." You could all choose a French name!

5

Comment tu t'appelles?
kom-*oh* too ta*pell*
What's your name?

6

Je m'appelle...
shj ma*pell*...
My name is...

7

Et toi?
ay twah
And you?

Choose a Name!

Alexandre
alex-*ahn*-dr

Nicolas
nee-kol-*ah*

Antoine
ahn-*twahn*

Thomas
toe-*mah*

Marie
ma-*ree*

Camille
kam-*eel*

Sarah
sah-*rah*

Manon
ma-*noh*

Quel âge as-tu?

You will need two dice for this game. One person throws them and the other asks **Quel âge as-tu?**
The dice thrower answers **J'ai… ans**, putting in the number the dice add up to. Take turns.

8

Quel âge as-tu?
kell ah-sh ah-too
How old are you?

9

J'ai neuf ans
shjay nehf ahn
I am nine years old

10

Bon anniversaire!
bon-anni-vair*sair*
Happy birthday!

Numbers! Numbers!

1	**un**	ahn		**7**	**sept**	set
2	**deux**	deuh		**8**	**huit**	weet
3	**trois**	trwah		**9**	**neuf**	nerf
4	**quatre**	katr'		**10**	**dix**	deess
5	**cinq**	sank		**11**	**onze**	onz
6	**six**	seess		**12**	**douze**	dooz

Look at the numbers on the inside front cover if you want to ask some older people their ages!

Ça va?

Cut out a circle of paper or card. Draw a smiley face on one side and a sad one on the other. Ask your friends **Ça va?** as you show them one of the faces. They have to try to give the right answer depending on if it is smiley or glum. Swap around so that you can practice too.

11

Ça va?
sa-vah
How are you?

12

Ça va bien, merci
sa-vah bee-ah mair-see
I'm fine, thanks

13

Ça ne va pas bien
sa neh vah *pah* bee-*eh*
I'm not so well

Words to Know	**Assez bien**	**Très bien**
	ah-*seh* bee-*eh*	treh bee-*eh*
Affreux	Quite well	Very good
ah-*freuh*		
Awful	**Comme ci comme ça**	**Merci**
	kom *see* kom *sah*	mair-*see*
	So-so	Thank you/thanks

9

Où est...?

Find all of the items in the **Words to Know** list and put them on a tray. Practice saying the French words for them. Now close your eyes while a friend takes one item off the tray. (Cover up the French words too.) You then have to ask **Où est le/la...?** whatever the missing thing is! Your friend will either say **Voilà le/la...** or **Encore une fois!** Take turns and try to remember.

14

Où est...?
oo ay
Where is...?

15

Voilà le/la...
wah-*lah* leh/lah
Here is the...

Encore une fois!
on-*kor* oon *fwah*
Try again!

A note about le and la
There are two words for "the" in French – **le** and **la**.
Try to learn them when you learn a new noun.

Words to Know

le livre
leh leevr'
book

le crayon
leh cray-*oh*
pencil

le crayon de couleur
leh cray-*oh* deh cool-*err*
colored pencil

la colle
lah koll
glue

le papier
leh papee-*eh*
paper

le stylo
leh steel*o*
pen

la gomme
lah gom
eraser

la règle
lah ray-gl'
ruler

Qu'est-ce que c'est?

Look at this outdoor scene and practice saying the French words. Then ask some friends or your family to play a drawing game with you. You each take turns drawing one of the named items and ask **Qu'est-ce-que c'est?** Everyone else has to try to say what it is from the drawing (and without looking at the French words). They say **C'est un/une....**

17

Qu'est-ce que c'est?
kes-keh seh
What is it?

une fille
oon fee
girl

un vélo
ahn vay*lo*
bicycle

un pique-nique
ahn peek-*neek*
picnic

12

un oiseau
ahn nwas-*o*
bird

un ballon
ahn ball*oh*
ball

18

C'est un/une...
set ahn/oon
It's a...

un sac à dos
ahn sak ah doh
backpack

un banc
ahn bah
bench

un garçon
ahn gar-*soh*
boy

A note about *un* and *une*
There are two words for "a" in French – **un** and **une**.
You say **C'est un** for a **le** word and **C'est une** for a
la word. For example, **C'est une fille** or **C'est un banc**.

Voici la famille

Spot the family! Look at page 15. Which four people are members of the same family? Point them out and say **Voici le fils** or **Voici la fille**. Use other words from **Words to Know** with **Voici** too. When you have found the whole family, you can say **Voici la famille**. Check your answers on page 32.

19

Voici le fils
vwah-*see* leh fees
Here's the son

20

Voici la fille
vwah-*see* lah fee
Here's the daughter

21

Voici la famille
vwah-*see* lah fam-*ee*
Here's the family

Words to Know

la mère/maman
lah mair/mam*ah*
mother/mom

le père/papa
leh pair/pa*pa*
father/dad

les parents
lay pah-*roh*
parents

la sœur
lah sir
sister

le frère
leh frair
brother

le bébé
leh beh-*beh*
baby

la grand-mère
lah groh-*mair*
grandmother

le grand-père
leh groh-*pair*
grandfather

15

J'aime...

Have a look at this picture and try to learn the French words for everything. Then choose four things you like and four you don't like. Practice saying if you like them or not by using the phrases **J'aime...** and **Je n'aime pas....** For example, **J'aime les fleurs** or **Je n'aime pas les moustiques**. Practice with a friend and take turns.

les chèvres
lay shevr
goats

les moustiques
lay mooss-*teek*
mosquitos

22

23

Je n'aime pas...
shj'*nem* pah
I don't like...

la pluie
lah ploo-ee
rain

J'aime...
shjem
I like...

les lapins
lay lah-*pah*
rabbits

les fleurs
lay fler
flowers

les chats
lay shah
cats

le soleil
leh so*lay*
sun

les arbres
lay *zar*-br'
trees

les canards
lay can-*ar*
ducks

les araignées
lay zaray-nee-*ay*
spiders

les cochons
lay koh-*shoh*
pigs

les chiens
lay shee-*yah*
dogs

Où habites-tu?

The children in the pictures are telling us where they live. Practice saying the phrases. Then cut out four pieces of paper to cover speech bubbles 25-28 and number them from 1 to 4. Ask a friend or adult to call out **un**, **deux**, **trois** or **quatre** and say **Où habites-tu?** You have to try to remember how to say where you live according to the scene next to the number.

24

Où habites-tu?
oo ab-eet too
Where do you live?

25

J'habite une maison
shja'beet oon meh-zoh
I live in a house

26

J'habite un appartement
shja'beet ahn appa-ter-moh
I live in an apartment

27

J'habite en ville
shja'*beet* ahn veel
I live in town

28

J'habite à la campagne
shja'*beet* ah lah kom-*pahn*-y'
I live in the country

Je voudrais...

Have some fun with this French shopping game for two or more people. Look at the shopping list and practice the words. The first player says **Je voudrais des pommes, s'il vous plaît,** and then points at the next thing on the list, the strawberries, on the market stall. The next player has to add them to the phrase, saying **Je voudrais des pommes et des fraises, s'il vous plaît.** Each player adds another thing to the list. The winner is the first one to say the whole list correctly. Then you can shout **C'est tout, merci.**

29

Je voudrais...
shj vood-*reh*
I would like...

30

S'il vous plaît
seel-voo-*pleh*
Please

31

C'est tout, merci
seh *too* mair-*see*
That's all, thanks

20

The Shopping List

des pommes
day pom
(some) apples

des fraises
day fraiz
(some) strawberries

des bananes
day ban-*an*
(some) bananas

des raisins
day ray-*zah*
(some) grapes

des carottes
day kah-*rot*
(some) carrots

des pommes de terre
day pom deh tair
(some) potatoes

des tomates
day tom-*aht*
(some) tomatoes

de la salade
deh lah sah-*lad*
(some) salad/lettuce

21

Un verre d'eau, s'il vous plaît

It's time to eat, so try asking for food and drink in French. You can ask a friend or adult to say **Qu'est-ce que tu veux?** All you need to do is choose something tasty from the menu and add **s'il vous plaît**. You might also like to say **J'ai faim** or **J'ai soif**.

32
Qu'est-ce que tu veux?
kes-keh too ver
What would you like?

33
J'ai faim
shjay *fa*
I'm hungry

34
J'ai soif
shjay *swaf*
I'm thirsty

35

Un verre d'eau,
s'il vous plaît
ahn vair doh seel-voo-*play*
A glass of water,
please

Menu/Le menu leh men-*oo*

un jus d'orange
ahn joo dor-*ronsh*
an orange juice

un verre d'eau
ahn vair doh
a glass of water

un verre de lait
ahn vair deh lay
a glass of milk

un morceau de gâteau
ahn morso deh gat-*oh*
a piece of cake

un yaourt
ahn yah-*oort*
a yogurt

des fruits
day froo-ee
some fruit

du pain
dew pan
some bread

du jambon
dew shjom*boh*
some ham

du fromage
dew from*ah-shj*
some cheese

des chips
day sheep
some potato chips

23

Qu'est-ce que tu veux faire?

You need two or more people to play this acting game.
Read the phrases and then cover them up. One of you
asks **Qu'est-ce que tu veux faire?** and acts out one
of the activities. The other player, or players, answer
Je veux... whatever they think the activity is.
Take turns being the actor.

36

Qu'est-ce que tu veux faire?
kes-keh too veh *fair*
What do you want to do?

37

Je veux regarder la télé
shj veh r'gar-*deh* lah teh-*leh*
I want to watch TV

38

Je veux jouer au football
shj veh shoo-eh oh foot*bol*
I want to play soccer

39

Je veux faire du vélo
shj veh *fair* doo *vay*lo
I want to ride a bike

40

Je veux nager
shj veh nah-*shay*
I want to go swimming

Words to Know

Tu veux…?
too veh
Do you want to…?

Oui, je veux bien
wee shj veh bee-*ah*
Yes, I'd like to

Non, merci
noh mair-*see*
No thanks

25

C'est de quelle couleur?

Here's a fun game to help you practice colors in French with your friends or family. You will need a die and some counters. When you land on a square all the other players shout **C'est de quelle couleur?** You say **Ma couleur préférée, c'est le rouge** or whatever color you have landed on. If you get the answer wrong you miss a turn. Good luck!

41

C'est de quelle couleur?
seh deh kel koo-*ler*
What color is it?

START

FINISH

42

Quelle est ta couleur préférée?
kel ay tah koo-*ler* prayfeh-*reh*
What's your favorite color?

Count in French
as you move
your counter.

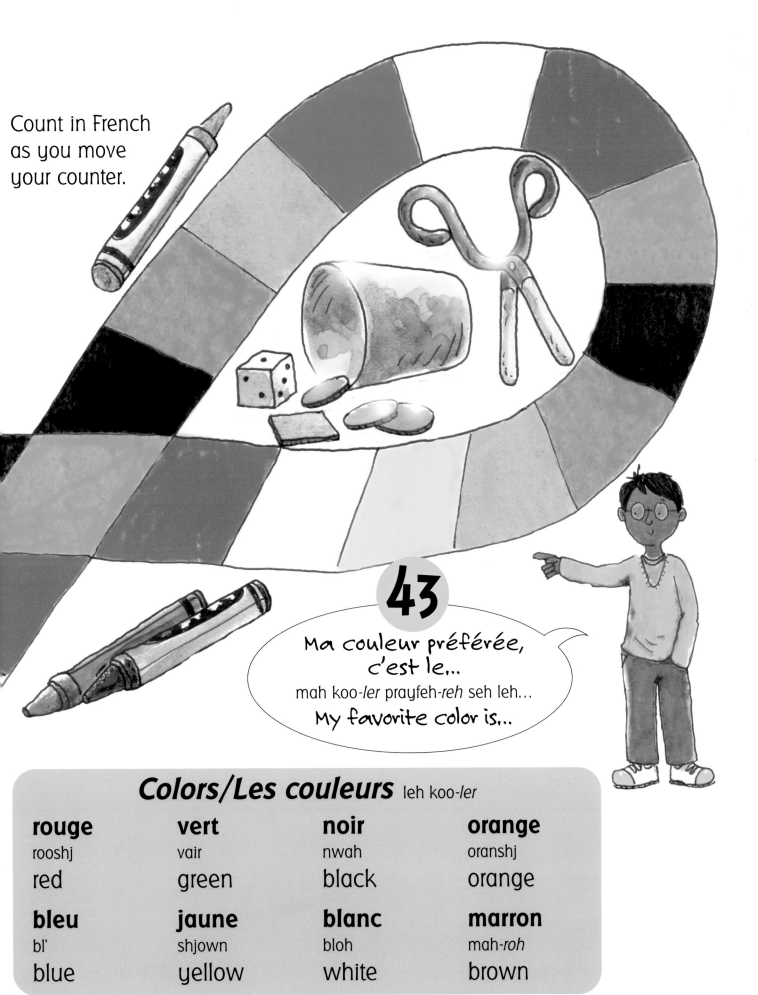

43

Ma couleur préférée,
c'est le...
mah koo-*ler* prayfeh-*reh* seh leh...
My favorite color is,...

Colors/Les couleurs leh koo-*ler*

rouge	**vert**	**noir**	**orange**
rooshj	vair	nwah	oranshj
red	green	black	orange
bleu	**jaune**	**blanc**	**marron**
bl'	shjown	bloh	mah-*roh*
blue	yellow	white	brown

Où vas-tu?

These children are all dressed for their vacations. See if you can match the right phrases to the children. Say **Où vas-tu?** and then choose the right answering phrase. Practice saying this out loud too. Check your answers on page 32.

44

Où vas-tu?
oo vah *too*
Where are you going?

45

Je vais à la plage
shj vay ah lah plah-shj
I'm going to the beach

46

Je vais à la campagne
shj vay ah lah kom-*pahn*-y'
I'm going to the country

47

Je vais à la montagne
shj vay ah lah mon-*tahn*-y'
I'm going to the mountains

48

Je vais en ville
shj vay ahn veel
I'm going to town

Words to Know

en vacances
ahn vak-*onss*
on vacation

Bon voyage!
boh vwoy-*ah-sh*
Have a good trip!

Je porte...

It is time to get dressed – in French! Have a look at the first picture and say **Je porte un petit pantalon**. Now look at the second picture and describe the difference in the pants. Say **Je porte un grand pantalon**. Continue describing the differences between the clothes on page 31. You'll need to use the **Words to Know** and have a look at the note about how to say "big" and "small" in French. You can check the answers on page 32.

49

Je porte un petit pantalon
shj port ahn p'tee pantah-*loh*
I'm wearing small pants

50

Je porte un grand pantalon
shj port ahn groh pantah-*loh*
I'm wearing big pants

Big or Small?

If the noun you are describing is a **le** word, you use **un grand** or **un petit**. If the noun is a **la** word, you use **une grande** or **une petite**. For example, **un grand manteau** or **une grande robe**; **un petit manteau** or **une petite robe**.

Words to Know

un pantalon	**un tee-shirt**	**une jupe**	**petit/petite**
ahn pantah-*loh*	ahn tee-*shairt*	oon shjoop	p'tee/p'-teet
pants	a T-shirt	a skirt	small
un manteau	**une casquette**	**un sweat**	**grand/grande**
ahn man-*toe*	oon kas*ket*	ahn swet	groh/grond
a coat	a cap	a sweatshirt	big

Solutions/Answers

Here are the answers to the activities on pages 2-3, 14-15, 28-29 and 30-31

pages 2-3

4 Bonne nuit

2 Au revoir

1 Bonjour

3 Bonsoir

pages 14-15

Voici la mère/ maman

Voici le grand-père

Voici la fille/ la sœur

Voici le fils/ le frère

pages 28-29

47 Je vais à la montagne

45 Je vais à la plage

48 Je vais en ville

46 Je vais à la campagne

pages 30-31

Je porte un grand manteau

Je porte un grand tee-shirt

Je porte une grande jupe

Je porte un grand sweat

Je porte une grande casquette

Je porte un petit manteau

Je porte un petit tee-shirt

Je porte une petite jupe

Je porte un petit sweat

Je porte une petite casquette

50 phrases français/50 French Phrases

1 **Bonjour** Hello, good morning

2 **Au revoir** Good-bye

3 **Bonsoir** Good evening

4 **Bonne nuit** Goodnight

5 **Comment tu t'appelles?** What's your name?

6 **Je m'appelle…** My name is…

7 **Et toi?** And you?

8 **Quel âge as-tu?** How old are you?

9 **J'ai neuf ans** I am nine years old

10 **Bon anniversaire!** Happy birthday!

11 **Ça va?** How are you?

12 **Ça va bien, merci** I'm fine, thanks

13 **Ça ne va pas bien** I'm not so well

14 **Où est…?** Where is…?

15 **Voilà le/la…** Here is the…

16 **Encore une fois!** Try again!

17 **Qu'est-ce que c'est?** What is it?

18 **C'est un/une…** It's a…

19 **Voici le fils** Here's the son

20 **Voici la fille** Here's the daughter

21 **Voici la famille** Here's the family

22 **J'aime…** I like…

23 **Je n'aime pas…** I don't like…

24 **Où habites-tu?** Where do you live?

25 **J'habite une maison** I live in a house

26 **J'habite un appartement** I live in an apartment

27 **J'habite en ville** I live in town

28 **J'habite à la campagne** I live in the country

29 **Je voudrais…** I would like…

30 **S'il vous plaît** Please

31 **C'est tout, merci** That's all, thanks

32 **Qu'est-ce que tu veux?** What would you like?

33 **J'ai faim** I'm hungry

34 **J'ai soif** I'm thirsty

35 **Un verre d'eau, s'il vous plaît** A glass of water, please

36 **Qu'est-ce que tu veux faire?** What do you want to do?

37 **Je veux regarder la télé** I want to watch TV

38 **Je veux jouer au football** I want to play soccer

39 **Je veux faire du vélo** I want to ride a bike

40 **Je veux nager** I want to go swimming

41 **C'est de quelle couleur?** What color is it?

42 **Quelle est ta couleur préférée?** What's your favorite color?

43 **Ma couleur préférée, c'est le…** My favorite color is…

44 **Où vas-tu?** Where are you going?

45 **Je vais à la plage** I'm going to the beach

46 **Je vais à la campagne** I'm going to the country

47 **Je vais à la montagne** I'm going to the mountains

48 **Je vais en ville** I'm going to town

49 **Je porte un petit pantalon** I'm wearing small pants

50 **Je porte un grand pantalon** I'm wearing big pants